COMMON ERRORS IN ENGLISH

G. CHRISTOPHER

Contents

About The Authors

Dr. Christopher, Dr. J. Anil Premraj and Dr. M.A. Mohamed Sahul Hameed have been teaching English at VIT University, Vellore for more than one and a half decades. Dr. J. Anil Premraj is heading the Dept. of English, VIT University, Vellore. The authors have published many research papers on language and literature in international journals of repute. They have received awards for their contributions to teaching and research. It is their unquenchable thirst for knowledge that has made this book see the light. The authors have attended several seminars, conferences, workshops, and training programs, and they have presented papers and delivered lectures on topics pertaining to teaching and research. They have organized many workshops in English for the benefit of the students and the teachers as well. They believe that the use of perfect English will be of immense benefit to the young learners in their academic and professional lives. The authors are always aware that they have more miles to go and more promises to keep.

Acknowledgements

'A favour done, not as return for another, is more valuable than heaven and earth put together.' – Thirukkural

Being believers ourselves, we, the authors offer our sincere prayers to God for His greatest blessings upon us! Nothing is possible without His Grace.

At the outset, we express our heartfelt thanks to our Hon'ble Chancellor Dr. G. Viswanathan, our respected Vice-Presidents Mr. Sankar Viswanathan, Dr. Sekar Viswanathan, and Dr. G.V. Selvam, and to our respected Vice-Chancellor, Dr. Kanchana Bhaaskaran, Pro Vice-Chancellor, Dr. Partha Sharathi Mallick, Registrar, Dr. T. Jayabarathi for their constant support and encouragement in bringing out this book to light.

We express a great deal of gratitude to Dr. M. Manoharan, Dean, Dr. V. Selvam, Associate Dean, all our beloved colleagues, Dept. of English, School of Social Sciences and Languages for their greatest support, timely help and motivation.

We thank Mr. M.S. Abdur Rahman, Research Assistant, Dept. of English, SSL, VIT University, Vellore for designing the cover page of the book, for making all page alignments and for helping us expeditiously bringing out this book to light.

Last but not the least, we profusely thank all our friends, well-wishers, research scholars, family members and dear and near ones for being with us in season and out of season. It is the fondness of our earnest and enthusiastic students that made us think of writing this book.

- Authors

Prologue

Our great freedom fighters struggled days and nights and underwent all sorts of trials and tribulations not to make the English quit but to make the English quit. The English left us but English stayed with us, continuing to enjoy a prestigious and privileged position among all our regional languages. Even though English seems to have its own domination over all languages of the world, it has never posed any threat to any language. The sun never sets on the British Empire and the sun never rises or sets on any country where there could be at least a few citizens without a good knowledge of English. Being an international language, it has its international importance. None on earth can pinpoint any field without the impact of the English language.

VIT University, despite being predominantly technical in nature always lays emphasis on the importance of English. Our Hon'ble Chancellor Dr. G. Viswanathan always insists on the chastity of the use of English. An English Proficiency Test (EPT) is conducted every year for students of all courses at the entry-level. One of the desirable objectives of our university is to produce excellent communicators in English.

Though errors are inevitable while using any language, too much of it is not desirable. It has its negative impact upon one who makes errors in language. While typing fast, typo errors might occur. There might occur grammatical errors, spelling mistakes and errors in the construction of sentences. Errors in informal communication might be tolerated or might leave unnoticed, but those in formal communication receive comments.

A little amount of accuracy while speaking a language could be sacrificed for the sake of fluency but errors while writing look quite glaring in the eyes of the readers. There are grammatically correct sentences but with ambiguity in meanings. There are verbally enriched sentences in written communication but not enhancing reading.

The purpose of the authors is not to locate all errors in the use of English but to make the learners aware of the errors that they might make while writing and to make them produce correct sentences to the maximum extent possible. Some of the common errors being made by non-native speakers of English are pinpointed and corrected through sample sentences. The authors will feel immensely satisfied when the young learners make their attempts meaningful by reading this book and finding it fruitful.

- Authors

CHAPTER ONE

ERRORS IN THE USE OF ARTICLES

(The articles 'a' and 'an' are called 'indefinite articles and 'the' is called the 'definite article'. The definite article 'the' is used when one talks about or makes a mention of someone or something specific or particular. 'a', 'e', 'i', 'o' and 'u' are the vowel letters in English, but the use of indefinite articles 'a' and 'an' is based on vowel sounds, not vowel letters.)

Dr Alexa is an university professor. (incorrect)

Dr Alexa is a university professor. (correct)

My neighbour's son is a M.Tech student. (incorrect)

My neighbour's son is an M.Tech student. (correct) (M-em)

A dinner that I had in my friend's house last night was fit for the gods. (incorrect)

The dinner that I had in my friend's house last night was fit for the gods.

Car that my daughter wishes to buy is Jaguar. (incorrect)

The car that my daughter wishes to buy is Jaguar. (correct)

Though Joe is an one- eyed man, he is a keen observer. (incorrect)

Though Joe is a one-eyed man, he is a keen observer. (correct)

Mr Mulrai, a ward member once, has now become the MP. (incorrect)

Mr Murali, a ward member once, has now become an MP. (correct)

Those two cars are ours; 110 is mine and 120 is my son's. (incorrect)

Those two cars are ours; the 110 is mine and the 120 is my son's.

I cannot sign this form without getting consent from officer concerned. (incorrect)

I cannot sign this form without getting consent from the officer concerned. (correct)

English are generally proud of their colour and heritage. (incorrect)

The English are generally proud of their colour and heritage. (correct)

('English' refers to the English language, whereas 'the English' refers to the English people (the British people.

The English is proud of his/her colour and heritage. (only one British man or a woman)

The English are proud of their colour and heritage. (The British people))

10.Juhi is tallest girl in my class. (incorrect)

Juhi is the tallest girl in my class. (correct)

('the' is used in superlative degree.)

11.White is a American but his cousin is a Australian. (incorrect)

White is an American and his cousin is an Australian. (correct)

12.Rohit will never forgive you for mistake that you have made. (incorrect)

Rohit will never forgive you for the mistake that you have made. (correct)

13.Poor are suffering everywhere because of skyrocketing price of essential commodities. (incorrect)

The poor are suffering everywhere because of the skyrocketing price of the essential commodities. (correct)

14.Nirad C. Chaudhuri is considered a eminent scholar in English. (incorrect)

Nirad C. Chaudhiri is considered an eminent scholar in English. (correct)

15.Satyam Computers has recently signed MoU with some foreign company. (incorrect)

Satyam Computers has recently signed an MoU with some foreign company. (correct)

16.Medicine that patient had last night, it seems, has some side effects. (incorrect)

The medicine that the patient had last night, it seems, has some side effects. (correct)

17.In spite of Johar being an European, he speaks and behaves as if he were a Indian. (incorrect)

In spite of Johar being a European, he speaks and behaves as if he were an Indian.

18.Dr Raghuram says that a L tube must have been used for an experiment. (incorrect)

Dr Raghuram says that an L tube must have been used for the experiment. (correct) (L-el)

19.What was time when your guest left for an airport? (incorrect)

What was the time when your guest left for the airport? (correct)

20.My grandmother told me a amazing story last night. (incorrect)

My grandmother told me an amazing story last night. (correct)

21.The officer, who was on duty, must shoulder responsibility for untoward incident that happened in our vicinity last night. (incorrect)

The officer, who was on duty, must shoulder responsibility for the untoward incident that happened in our vicinity last night. (correct)

22.Black are still being ill-treated by White in some countries. (incorrect)

The black are still being ill-treated by the White in some countries. (correct)

('The Black' refers to 'the black people, and 'the White' refers to 'the White people'. When there two persons with names Black and White, it can be said, "Black is being ill-treated by White.)

23.Third person in line seems to be fit for job. (incorrect)

The third person in the line seems to be fit for the job. (correct)

24.Tomy is a absent-minded professor. (incorrect)

Tomy is an absent-minded professor. (correct)

25.Hands that help are holier than lips that pray. (incorrect)

The hands that help are holier than the lips that pray. (correct)

CHAPTER TWO

ERRORS IN THE USE OF PREPOSITIONS

1.Charles is talking to Lucy through phone now. (incorrect)

Charles is talking to Lucy over/on phone now. (correct)

2.What's the time in your watch now? (incorrect)

What's the time by your watch now? (correct)

3.The patient is taking rest now in the advice of the doctor now. (incorrect)

The patient is taking rest now on the advice of the doctor now. (correct)

4.My maternal uncle is in abroad. (incorrect)

My maternal uncle is abroad. (correct)

5.Mr Albert asks his students to go to downstairs for the next class. (incorrect)

Mr Albert asks his students to go downstairs for the next class. (correct)

6.The MLA is not known even by the people of his own constituency. (incorrect)

The MLA is not known even to the people of his own constituency. (correct)

7.Nilofer has known Sameel in the past 7 years. (incorrect)

Nilofer has known sameel for the past 7 years. (correct)

8.In the instruction from the Director, the order was issued last night. (incorrect)

On the instruction from the Director, the order was issued last night. (correct)

9.Aju has invited all his friends for his sister's marriage. (incorrect)

Aju has invited all his friends to his sister's marriage. (correct)

10.All parties had a lot of discussion with the issue last week. (incorrect)

All parties had a lot of discussion on/over the issue last week. (correct)

11.The chief guest is introduced by Miss Menaka for the audience. (incorrect)

The chief guest is introduced by Miss Menaka to the audience. (correct)

12.Tiwari was late to exam hall this morning in 10 minutes. (incorrect)

Tiwari was late to exam hall this morning by 10 minutes. (correct)

13.Much annoyed by some issue, James looks dull. (incorrect)

Much annoyed over some issue, James looks dull. (correct)

14.There are several brickbats thrown on the politician with his political rivals. (incorrect)

There are several brickbats thrown at the politician by his political rivals. (correct)

15.All party leaders stand united for their determination to defenestrate their common political rival. (incorrect)

All party leaders stand united in their determination to defenestrate their common political rival. (correct)

16.The employees are loyal for their boss. (incorrect)

The employees are loyal to their boss. (correct)

17.Dr Sherin is the author for 145 books about ornithology. (incorrect)

Dr Sherin is the author of 145 books on ornithology. (correct)

18.Diana is making a presentation now in the topic 'How to develop administrative skills?'. (incorrect)

Diana is making a presentation now on the topic 'How to develop administrative skills?'. (correct)

19.The IAS officer says that the accusations of the press with him are a farrago of lies. (incorrect)

The IAS officer says that the accusations of the press against him are a farrago of lies. (correct)

20.You cannot trust Samuel by any secret. (incorrect)

You cannot trust Samuel with any secret. (correct)

21.The orator is never on the loss with words. (incorrect)

The orator is never at loss for words. (correct)

22.My friend is a born Luddite and so you cannot convert him to a great technologist. (incorrect)

My friend is a born Luddite and so you cannot convert him into a great technologist. (correct)

23.All his qualities are associated by muliebrity. (incorrect)

All his qualities are associated with muliebrity. (correct)

24.Albert Einstein's contributions for science are commendable. (incorrect)

Albert Einstein's contributions to science are commendable. (correct)

25.I shall accompany with you to the theatre this evening. (incorrect)

I shall accompany you to the theatre this evening. (correct)

CHAPTER THREE

ERRORS IN THE USE OF TENSES

1.Prof Taram Singh teaches his students poetry now. (incorrect)

Prof Taram Singh is teaching his students poetry now. (correct)

2.Next week by this time, I shall travel to Iraq. (incorrect)

Next week by this time, I shall have been traveling to Iraq. (correct)

3.Next week by this time, the candidate will submit his PhD thesis. (incorrect)

Next week by this time, the candidate will have submitted his PhD thesis. (correct)

4.Tom is living in London since 1997. (incorrect)

Tom has been living in London since 1997. (correct)

5.I have been knowing Tom since 1997. (incorrect)

I have known Tom since 1997. (correct)

6.Prof Kailash will take class between 9: 00 and 10:00 AM tomorrow. (incorrect)

Prof Kailash will be taking class between 9:00 and 10:00 AM tomorrow. (correct)

7.I was writing a letter to my dad last month, asking him for money, but I did not receive from him any amount yet. (incorrect)

I wrote a letter to my dad last month, asking him for money, but I have not yet received from him any amount. (correct)

8.The thief has been caught last night and the police has been searching for him for the past 7 years. (incorrect)

The thief was caught last night, and the police had been searching for him for the past 7 years. (correct)

9.The thief had not been caught yet and the police had been searching for him for the 7 years. (incorrect)

The thief has not yet been caught and the police have been searching for him for the past 7 years. (correct)

10.All that glitters was not gold. (incorrect)

All that glitters is not gold. (correct)

11.I am going to bed at 10 PM every night. (incorrect)

I go to bed at 10 PM every night. (correct)

12.Before my guest reached the station last evening, the train left. (incorrect)

Before my guest reached the station last evening, the train had left. (correct)

13.On the advice of the doctor, the patient takes rest now. (incorrect)

On the advice of the doctor, the patient is taking rest now. (correct)

14.When my friends had come to our house yesterday, my mother prepared food for them. (incorrect)

When my friends came to our house yesterday, my mother was preparing food for them. (correct)

15.As soon as the collector heard the news this morning, he was rushing to the spot. (incorrect)

As soon as the collector heard the news this morning, he rushed to the spot. (correct)

16.Dr Kurian produced 23 PhDs so far. (incorrect)

Dr Kurian has produced 23 PhD s so far. (correct)

17.Had the minister been informed of the programme earlier, he would grace it with his presence. (incorrect)

Had the minister been informed of the programme earlier, he would have graced it with his presence. (correct)

18.I have had a nice dream last night. (incorrect)

I had a dream last night. (correct)

19.The patient died even before the operation was performed. (incorrect)

The patient had died even before the operation was performed. (correct)

20.The team is working on this project for more than three years. (incorrect)

The team has been working on this project for more than three years. (correct)

21.Our businessman is never making any compromise in matters of quality. (incorrect)

Our businessman never makes any compromise in matters of quality. (correct)

22.Why did you not submitted your assignment yet? (incorrect)

Why have you not submitted your assignment yet? (correct)

23.Toru is always speaking the truth. (incorrect)

Toru always speaks the truth. (correct)

24.I shall be meeting you tomorrow. (incorrect)

I shall meet you tomorrow. (correct)

25.I had gone to the railway station yesterday. The station master told me that the timetable was altered the previous week. (incorrect)

I went to the railway station yesterday. The station master told me that the timetable had been altered the previous week. (correct)

CHAPTER FOUR

ERRORS IN SUBJECT-VERB AGREEMENT (CONCORD)

1.Tony along with his wife and children are going to Ooty during summer vacation. (incorrect)

Tony along with his wife and children is going to Ooty during summer vacation. (correct)

2.My testimonials along with other testimonials are enclosed for your perusal. (incorrect)

My testimonials along with other testimonials is enclosed for your perusal. (correct)

3.Neither the labourers nor their union leader are responsible for the strike. (incorrect)

Neither the labourers nor their union leader is responsible for the strike. (correct)

4.Neither their union leader nor the labourers is responsible for the strike. (incorrect)

Neither their union leader nor the labourers are responsible for the strike. (correct)

5.The police suspect that either Tom or his two brothers is at fault. (incorrect)

The police suspect that either Tom or his two brothers are at fault. (correct)

6.One of the Oxford University professors are a good friend of mine. (incorrect)

One of the Oxford University professors is a good friend of mine. (correct)

7.All these equipment is available in our laboratory. (incorrect)

All these equipment are available in our laboratory. (correct)

8.These news is not reliable. (incorrect)

These news are not reliable. (correct)

9.These information are obtained from some reliable sources. (incorrect)

These information are obtained from some reliable sources. (correct)

10.Banu as well her brothers have joined the TOEFL course. (incorrect)

Banu as well as her brothers has joined the TOEFL course. (correct)

11.Peter's children as well as his neighbour's son wishes to win the race. (incorrect)

Peter's children as well as his neighbour's son wish to win the race. (correct)

12.The principal and class teacher are going rounds now. (incorrect)

The principal and class teacher is going rounds now. (correct)

13.The principal and the class teacher is going rounds now. (incorrect)

The principal and the class teacher are going rounds now. (correct)

14.The students say that of all the grammar components, 'Tenses' make one tense. (incorrect)

The students say that of all the grammar components, 'Tenses' makes one tense. (correct)

15.One of the main reasons for frequent road accidents are use of mobile phones while driving. (incorrect)

One of the main reasons for frequent road accidents is use of mobile phones while driving. (correct)

16.The politician, on the advice of his doctors, are taking rest now. (incorrect)

The politician, on the advice of his doctors, is taking rest now. (correct)

17.Two hours are not a long duration for conducting such examinations. (incorrect)

Two hours is not a long duration for conducting such examinations. (correct)

18.The book that contains 15 chapters are interesting. (incorrect)

The book that contains 15 chapters is interesting. (correct)

19.The United States of America have spent billions and billions on this project. (incorrect)

The United States of America has spent billions and billions on this project. (correct)

20.Each and every one of them are responsible for the untoward incident that happened in the city last night. (incorrect)

Each and every one of them is responsible for the untoward incident that happened in the city last night.

(correct)

21.Bread and butter are good during journeys. (incorrect)

Bread and butter is good during journeys. (correct)

22.Nilofer is one of the officers who has been recently elevated to the next cadre. (incorrect)

Nilofer is one of the officers who have been recently elevated to the next cadre. (correct)

23.Many a teacher are honoured on Teachers' Day this year. (incorrect)

Many a teacher is honoured on the Teachers' Day this year. (correct)

24.'We' are the subject of the sentence 'We are playing cricket now'. (incorrect)

'We' is the subject of the sentence 'We are playing cricket now'. (correct)

25.The committee comprising of 15 members have not yet arrived at a decision. (incorrect)

The committee comprising of 15 members has not yet arrived at a decision. (correct)

CHAPTER FIVE

CONNECTIVES

If I went to my friend's house, his mother was preparing food. (incorrect)

When I went to my friend's house, his mother was preparing food. (correct)

No sooner did he receive the message, he started. (incorrect)

No sooner did he receive the message than he started. (correct)

Even though my neighbours are living in abject penury, but they are quite happy. (incorrect)

Even though my neighbours are living in abject penury, they are quite happy.

Hardly had the collector got the news of bomb explosion in the tense area, he rushed to the spot. (incorrect)

Hardly had the collector got the news of bomb explosion in the tense area, when he rushed to the spot. (correct)

Meena was very happy that she forgot to have her breakfast and lunch. (incorrect)

Meena was so happy that she forgot to have her breakfast and lunch. (correct)

As long as he was rich, till then he was surrounded by a number of friends. (incorrect)

As long as he was rich, he was surrounded by a number of friends. (correct)

If Arun meets the minister and gets a recommendation letter, only then he can get this job. (incorrect)

If Arun meets the minister and gets a recommendation letter, he can get this job.

Before I reached the airport last night, the guest left. (correct)

Before I reached the airport last night, the guest had left. (correct)

Since Seshadri is not well, so he had made some alternative arrangements for his classes. (incorrect)

Since Seshadri is not well, he has made some alternative arrangements for his classes. (correct)

No sentence ends with 'because', 'because' is a conjunction. (incorrect)

No sentence ends with 'because', because 'because' is a conjunction. (correct)

As there was a heavy traffic congestion, that was the reason why I could not reach the auditorium on time. (incorrect)

As there was a heavy traffic congestion, I could not reach the auditorium on time. (correct)

Though Varun performed well in the interview, but he was not selected. (incorrect)

Though Varun performed well in the interview, he was not selected. (correct)

Unless you have a lot of practice, you cannot develop your communication skills otherwise. (incorrect)

Unless you have a lot of practice, you cannot develop your communication skills. (correct)

Because the project is expensive, so the govt assistance is necessary. (incorrect)

Because the project is expensive, the govt assistance is necessary. (correct)

After the speaker delivered lecture for three hours, he took complete rest. (incorrect)

After the speaker had delivered lecture for three hours, he took complete rest. (correct)

If the team had not completed the project on time, they will not get approval for the second project. (incorrect)

If the team does not complete the project on time, they will not gct approval for the second project. (correct)

As Raja is the richest in our district, that is why he is happy and arrogant. (incorrect)

As Raja is the richest in our district, he is happy and arrogant. (correct)

If the leader had been arrested, the people would indulge in violence. (incorrect)

If the leader had been arrested, the people would have indulged in violence. (correct)

When the professor entered the class, that time Kumar was sleeping in the last row. (incorrect)

When the professor entered the class, Kumar was sleeping in the last row. (correct)

Although everything is spick and span, but the manager tries to pick holes in everyone's coat. (incorrect)

Although everything is spick and span, the manager tries to pick holes in everyone's coat. (correct)

CHAPTER SIX

ERRORS IN CONDITIONALS

If I was in your position, I will help the poor. (wrong)

If I were in your position, I would help the poor. (correct)

Had you contacted him, he would help you. (wrong)

Had you contacted him, he would have helped you. (correct)

If proper plans had made, the businessman would have come off with flying colours. (wrong)

If proper plans had been made, the businessman would have come off with flying colours. (correct)

If you run fast, you would have caught the train. (wrong)

If you run fast, you will catch the train. (correct)

Unless you fulfil the requirements, you would not have been considered for the post. (wrong)

Unless you fulfil the requirements, you will not be considered for the post. (correct)

If you read great writers like Nehru, you would have enhanced your writing skills. (wrong)

If you read great writers like Nehru, you can enhance your writing skills. (correct)

If she work on this project, she may definitely get some experience. (wrong)

If she works on this project, she may get some experience. (correct)

Even if he is an actor, he would not have earned money. (wrong)

Even if he were an actor, he would not earn money. (correct)

If Seshadri had been a teacher, he will produce wonderful students. (wrong)

If Seshadri had been a teacher, he would have produced wonderful students. (correct)

If all great books were translated into English, the world will benefit a lot. (wrong)

If all great books were translated into English, the world would benefit a lot. (correct)

If you are coming to my house, I shall give you some books. (wrong)

If you come to my house, I shall give you some books. (correct)

Unless you repeat what you said, your students would not have understood the subject. (wrong)

Unless you repeat what, you said, your students will not understand the subject. (correct)

Unless you lose something at least once, you would not have thought of winning everything. (wrong)

Unless you lose something at least once, you cannot think of winning everything. (correct)

What would happen, if you had not attended the interview? (wrong)

What would have happened if you had not attended the interview? (correct)

If he knows the truth, he would have revealed it in the court. (wrong)

If he knows the truth, he will reveal it in the court. (correct)

If all the products had sold out, he would have continued his business. (wrong)

If all the products had been sold out, he would have continued his business. (correct)

If Arun gets a recommendation letter from the PWD minister, he would get the job easily. (wrong)

If Arun gets a recommendation letter from the PWD minister, he will get the job easily. (correct)

Varun's life will be happier, had he married Visalini. (wrong)

Vraun's life would have been happier, had he married Visalini. (correct)

If you developed your communication skills in English, you will get a good job. (wrong)

If you develop your communication skills in English, you will get a good job. (correct)

Would you be happy if I meet you every day? (wrong)

Would you be happy if I met you every day? (correct)

Had you completed mock interview, the teacher will not scold you. (incorrect)

Had you completed mock interview, the teacher would not have scolded you.

Were I one of the judges, I will choose you for the final round. (incorrect)

Were I one of the judges, I would choose you for the final round. (correct)

If Menaka had joined the team, the project proposal will have come up well. (incorrect)

If Menaka had joined the team, the project proposal would have come up well. (correct)

All students will benefit a lot, if a good researcher had appointed as a faculty member. (incorrect)

All students will benefit a lot, if a good researcher is appointed as a member of faculty. (correct)

If the institute had recognized the knowledgeable teachers and researchers, the quality will be good. (incorrect)

If the institute had recognized the knowledgeable teachers and researchers, the quality would have been good. (correct)

CHAPTER SEVEN

ERRORS IN DIRECT-INDIRECT SPEECH FORMS

Nilofer told that she will present a paper in the conference tomorrow. (incorrect)

Nilofer said that she would present a paper in the conference the next day. (correct)

The teacher said that the sun rose in the east set in the west. (correct)

The teacher said that the sun rises in the east and sets in the west. (Universal/ Permanent truths are expressed in Present Tense.)

The manager told to me to completed the work within two hours. (incorrect)

The manager asked me to complete the work within two hours. (correct)

Suresh kindly requested Mohan to offer to him an opportunity to work in his company. (incorrect)

Suresh requested Mohan to offer him an opportunity to work in his company. (correct)

The foreign leaders exclaimed if the Taj Mahal was beautiful. (incorrect)

The foreign leaders exclaimed that the Taj Mahal was very beautiful. (correct)

Baskar asked to Balu weather he could help him upload his assignments. (incorrect)

Baskar asked Balu whether he could help him upload his assignments. (correct)

Varun asked Divya if how was she. (incorrect)

Varun asked Divya how she was. (correct)

Arun asked to his friend if he can come to his house today. (incorrect)

Arun asked his friend if he could come to his house that day. (correct)

Our class teacher told to us that there will be inspection tomorrow. (incorrect)

Our class teacher told us that there would be inspection the next day. (correct)

Our science teacher said that internet was a great boon. (incorrect)

Our teacher said that internet is a great boon. (correct)

Dr Aniruth said that he is too busy that he cannot guide anyone this year. (incorrect)

Dr Aniruth said that he was too busy to guide anyone that year. (correct)

The doctor adviced to the patient to take rest for two weeks. (incorrect)

The doctor advised the patient to take rest for two weeks. (correct)

Ram told Rahim that they can go to school together everyday. (incorrect)

Ram told Rahim that they could go to school together every day. (correct)

The politician told the people of his constituency that he will not meet them on five years. (incorrect)

The politician told the people of his constituency that he would not meet them for five years. (correct)

Kumar asked his friend how he can he speak like this. (incorrect)

Kumar asked his friend how he could speak like that. (correct)

My daughter says that she wished to become a IAS officer. (incorrect)

My daughter says that she wishes to become an IAS officer. (correct)

The station master told the passengers that the timetable was altered last week. (incorrect)

The station master told the passengers that the timetable had been altered the previous week. (correct)

The MD ordered to his peon to kept all the files on his table before 5 PM today. (incorrect)

The MD ordered his peon to keep all the files on his table before 5 PM that day. (correct)

My mother says me to work hard. (incorrect)

My mother advises me to work hard. (correct)

The speaker told the audience that he feels sorry for making them to wait for a long time. (incorrect)

The speaker told the audience that he felt sorry for making them wait for a long time. (correct)

The police told to the accused that he may produce him in the court next week. (incorrect)

The police told the accused that he might produce him in the court the coming week. (correct)

Prakash said that the leader does not raise his voice in the meeting. (incorrect)

Prakash said that the leader did not raise his voice in the meeting. (correct)

The interviewer asked to the candidate where are you from?. (incorrect)

The interviewer asked the candidate where he/she was from. (correct)

The team leader said them to hold negotiation with the company authorities. (incorrect)

The team leader asked them to hold negotiation with the company authorities. (correct)

I said to my father that I will get my paper publish in one or two weaks. (incorrect)

I told my father that I would get my paper published in one or two weeks.

CHAPTER EIGHT

ERRORS IN THE USE OF VOICE FORMS (ACTIVE & PASSIVE)

Sunil got his progress card last week, but he has not yet showed it to his parents. (wrong)

Sunil got his progress card last week, but he has not yet shown it to his parents. (correct)

Tom has putted forth the maximum efforts to win the game. (wrong)

Tom has put forth the maximum efforts to win the game. (correct)

Dr Rufus is well-known by all international businessmen. (wrong)

Dr Rufus is well-known to all international businessmen. (correct)

This work is done by me continuously. (wrong)

This work is being done by me continuously. (correct)

What is known by me is known by you. (wrong)

What is known to me is known to you. (correct)
The picture is looked by the children. (wrong)
The picture is looked at by the children. (correct)
The lecture is listened by all students now. (wrong)
The lecture is being listened to by all students now. (correct)
The door is knocked by someone. (wrong)
The door is knocked at by someone. (correct)
They all mock him for no reason. (wrong)
They all mock at him for no reason. (correct)
Is Man laughed by other creatures? (wrong)
Is Man laughed at by other creatures? (correct)
What is proposal is disposed by God. (wrong)
What is proposed is disposed by God. (correct)
The police caught him last night, but no action is taken against him yet. (wrong)
The police caught him last night, but no action has been yet taken against him. (correct)
Next week by this time, the thesis will be submitted to the office. (wrong)
Next week by this time, the thesis will have been submitted to the office. (correct)
These supports bearings are called. (wrong and incomplete)
These supports are called bearings. (correct)
The live electric wire should not touch by him. (wrong)
The live electric wire should not be touched. (correct)
The operation is performed now. (wrong)
The operation is being performed now. (correct)
The criminal is beated by the police black and blue. (wrong)
The criminal is beaten black and blue by the police. (correct)

We have casted our votes for the party. (wrong)

We have cast our votes for the party. (correct)

He will never be letted down. (wrong)

He will never be let down. (correct)

The concept was being well-understood by all students. (wrong)

The concept was well-understood by all students. (correct)

The news was being hearded and immediately the collector was rushing to the spot. (wrong)

The news was heard and immediately the collector rushed to the spot. (correct)

The article was not properly readed by any student. (wrong)

The articled was not properly read by any student. (correct)

The faithful are never forsaked by the Almighty. (wrong)

The faithful are never forsaken by the Almighty.

All sins are forgived by God. (wrong)

All sins are forgiven by God. (correct)

The guests were welcome by the minister with open arms last night at the airport. (wrong)

The guests were welcomed by the minister with the open arms last night. (correct)

CHAPTER NINE

ERRORS IN THE USE OF QUESTIONS

He is a rich man, is it? (incorrect)

He is a rich man, isn't it?

David cannot solve this problem, isn't it? (incorrect)

David cannot solve this problem, can he? (correct)

Some of the students have not uploaded their assignments, aren't they? (incorrect)

Some of the students have not uploaded their assignments, have they? (correct)

They are playing cricket now, are they? (incorrect)

They are playing cricket now, aren't they? (correct)

Time and tide wait for none, isn't it? (incorrect)

Time and tide wait for none, don't they? (correct)

Sujid is not doing business, is he doing? (incorrect)

Sujid is not doing business, is he? (correct)

We prefer coffee to tea, right. (incorrect)

We prefer coffee to tea, don't we? (correct)

Diana is the milk of human kindness, is she? (incorrect)

Diana is the milk of human kindness, isn't she? (correct)

Albert is guiding six research scholars now, am I? (incorrect)

Albert is guiding six scholars now, isn't he? (correct)

How you completed your work on time? (incorrect)

How did you complete your work on time? (correct)

How long you will stay in Ooty? (incorrect)

How long will you stay in Ooty/ (correct)

Why you are late. (incorrect)

Why are you late? (correct)

Did you ever expected that this would happen? (incorrect)

Did you ever expect that this would happen? (correct)

You have not hurt the feelings of your colleagues even once, isn't it? (incorrect)

You have not hurt the feelings of your colleagues even once, have you? (correct)

Meena has not given her consent to marry Tarun, is it? (incorrect)

Meena has not given her consent to marry Tarun, has she? (correct)

You do not know how to solve this problem, don't you? (incorrect)

You do not know how to solve this problem, do you? (correct)

This officer is very strict, isn't it? (incorrect)

This officer is very strict, is he/she?

Roses are beautiful, isn't it? (incorrect)

Roses are beautiful, aren't they? (correct)

The doctor congratulated her daughter on her success in the IAS exam, is it? (incorrect)

The doctor congratulated her daughter on her success in the IAS exam, didn't she? (correct)

Prevention is better than cure, is it? (incorrect)

Prevention is better than cure, isn't it? (correct)

Coming events cast their shadows before, do it? (incorrect)

Coming events cast their shadows before, don't they? (correct)

Arun has bought a new car, isn't it? (incorrect)

Arun has bought a new car, hasn't he? (correct)

Ravi met all his old classmates in Delhi last week, isn't he? (incorrect)

Ravi met all his old classmates in Delhi last week, didn't he? (correct)

They are Kamal's fans, is it? (incorrect)

They are Kamal's fans, aren't they? (correct)

The candidate has not performed well in the interview, is he? (incorrect)

The candidate has not performed well in the interview, has he/she? (correct)

CHAPTER TEN

SPELLING ERRORS

This is the nineth time that Tom has applied for the post. (incorrect)

This is the ninth time that Tom has applied for the post. (correct)

Your talk on the issue has caused a great embarasment to your colleagues. (incorrect)

Your talk on the issue has caused a great embarrassment to your colleagues. (correct)

Naveen has been appointed as Sperindent of Police of our District. (incorrect)

Naveen has been appointed as Superintendent of police of our District. (correct)

Communication skills can be developed by means of constant practise. (incorrect)

Communication skills can be developed by means of constant practice. (correct)

His advise has fallen on his son's deaf ears. (incorrect)

His advice has fallen on his son's deaf ears. (correct)

I do not no who you are. (incorrect)

I do not know who you are. (correct)

Ashwitha is a Member of parliment. (incorrect)

Ashwitha is a Memebr of Parliament. (correct)

Liyodi has been suffering from nimonia for the past three weeks. (incorrect)

Liyodi has been suffering from pneumonia for the past three weeks (correct)

Revathy is too week in English to teach even Pre-KG children. (incorrect)

Revathy is too weak in English to teach even Pre-KG children. (correct)

The minister says that he does not won a car. (incorrect)

The minister says that he does not own a car. (correct)

The soldiers have own the battle. (incorrect)

The soldiers have won the battle. (correct)

The manager says that he cannot soldier responsibility for the loss. (incorrect)

The manager says that he cannot shoulder responsibility for the loss. (correct)

There are tution centres everywehere to teach spellings. (incorrect)

There are tuition centres everywhere to teach spellings. (correct)

Walls have years. (incorrect)

Walls have ears. (correct)

Hyginic food is available here. (incorrect)

Hygienic food is available here. (correct)

A number of foriners visit India for the programme this year. (incorrect)

A nember of foreigners visit India for the programme this year. (correct)

The minister says that he will meat the people every day. (incorrect)

The minister says that he will meet the people every day. (correct)

The comiti will take some suitable decision soon. (incorrect)

The committee will take some suitable decision soon. (correct)

The file contains the minits of the meeting. (incorrect)

The file contains the minutes of the meeting. (correct)

We will cost our votes for the party. (incorrect)

We will cast our votes for the party. (correct)

This type of building will cast you more. (incorrect)

This type of building will cost you more. (correct)

The student says that he goes to collage every day by car. (incorrect)

The student says that he goes to college every day by car. (correct)

There is no acomodation in the hostel. (incorrect)

There is no accommodation in the hostel. (correct)

I read Shakespeare's 'Twelth Night' last night. (incorrect)

I read Shakespeare's 'Twelfth Night' last night.

By reading many books, he is becoming encyklopadic. (incorrect)

By reading many books, he is becoming encyclopedic. (correct)

CHAPTER ELEVEN

COMMON ERRORS

The team members on the advise of the leader has made a few changes on their new project proposal. (incorrect)

The team members, on the advice of the leader, have made a few changes on their new project proposal. (correct)

Either the officers or the Commissioner have to shoulder responsibility for the untoward incident that happened in Karim Nagar last Thursday. (incorrect)

Either the officers or the Commissioner has to shoulder responsibility for the untoward incident that happened in Karim Nagar last Thursday. (correct)

Because of the Chairman has his heart in the right place, all officers like him. (incorrect)

Because the Chairman has his heart in the right place, all officers like him. (correct)

The young lawyer is practicing the argumentative skills now under the able guidance of the retired judge. (incorrect)

The young lawyer is practising the argumentative skills now under the able guidance of the retired judge. (correct)

The number of participants in the Literature Festival were more than 300. (incorrect)

The number of participants in the Literature Festival was more than 300. (correct)

Ram asked his boss when will he be sent to Singapore for material collection. (incorrect)

Ram asked his boss when he will be sent to Singapore for material collection. (correct)

The weather in Ooty is as pleasant as Kodaikanal. (incorrect)

The weather in Ooty is as pleasant as that in Kodaikanal. (correct)

The Govt is planning to implement the new schemes. (incorrect)

The Govt is planning to implement the new schemes. (correct)

The corrupt officer was outed out from service. (incorrect)

The corrupt officer was outed from service last week. (correct) (Time to be mentioned.)

The principal said that the students of nineth std threw stones on the glass. (incorrect)

The principal said that the students of ninth std had thrown stones on the glass. (correct) (Std IX)

The collector insisted his secretary to keep the report ready. (incorrect)

The collector insisted on his secretary keeping the report ready. (correct)

The collector insisted that his secretary keep the report ready. (correct) (not keeps)

The collector insisted that the report be kept by his secretary ready. (correct)

The lawyer suggested his client to produce the evidence before the next hearing. (incorrect)

The lawyer suggested that his client produce the evidence before the next hearing. (correct) (could produce)

The lawyer suggested to his client that the evidence be produced before the next hearing. (correct)

I wish you will do your best as our representative in the council meeting. (incorrect)

I wish that you did (would/could/might do) your best as our representative in the council meeting. (correct)

The problem is too complicated that the young man cannot find a solution. (incorrect)

The problem is so complicated that the young man cannot find a solution. (correct)

The problem is too complicated for the young man to find a solution. (correct)

It is high time that ward member must visit the poorly maintained streets. (incorrect)

It is high time that the ward member visited the poorly maintained streets. (correct)

Not withstanding the fact that his status being low, all respect him. (incorrect)

Notwithstanding his economic status being low, all respect him. (correct)

Notwithstanding the fact that his economic status is low, all respect him. (correct)

The books were not referred by the researcher. (incorrect)

The books were not referred to by the researcher. (correct)

Those who did not upload the assignments on time they will not be allowed to appear for the final exam. (incorrect)

Those, who did not upload the assignments on time, will not be allowed to appear for the final exam. (correct)

Hardly had he received the report, he ordered to arrest the culprits. (incorrect)

Hardly had he received the report when he ordered that the culprits be arrested. (correct)

I kindly request to forward the proposal to the concerned officer within a week. (incorrect)

I request you to forward the proposal to the officer concerned within a week. (correct)

Toru was depromoted because of his negligence of duty. (incorrect)

Toru was demoted because of his negligence of duty. (correct)

The minister had an appointment with the Governor between 10 to 10:30 AM last week. (incorrect)

The minister had an appointment with the Governor between 10:00 and 10:30 AM last week.

Mithun insists his daughter to become an IAS officer. (incorrect)

Mithun insists on his daughter becoming an IAS officer. (correct)

Mithun insists that his daughter become an IAS officer. (correct)

Bread and butter are good during journeys. (incorrect)

Bread and butter is good during journeys. (correct)

Both bread and butter is available in this shop. (incorrect)

Both bread and butter are available in this shop. (correct)

After making the purchase, I paid the amount by cash. (incorrect)

After making the purchase, I paid in cash. (correct)

After making the purchase, I paid the cash. (correct)

After making the purchase, I paid in credit card. (incorrect)

After making the purchase, I paid by credit card. (correct)

My grandfather walks in the mornings everyday. (incorrect).

My grandfather walks in the morning every day. (correct)

Despite of being a professor for a long period, Revathy could not improve her knowledge of grammar. (incorrect)

Despite being a professor for a long period, Revathy could not improve her knowledge of grammar. (correct)

Even though Some is a school dropout, he has got patent for his product. (incorrect)

Even though Somu is a school dropout, he has got patent for his product. (correct)

Ritu got her progress card last month, but she has not yet showed it to her father. (incorrect)

Ritu got her progress card last month, but she has not yet shown it to her father. (correct)

The candidate joined duty in the forenoon of today. (incorrect)

The candidate joined duty on the forenoon of today. (correct)

My sister accompanied with me to theatre last evening. (incorrect)

My sister accompanied me to the theatre last evening. (correct)

Sita is my cousin sister. (incorrect)

Sita is my cousin. (correct)

My uncle is in abroad. (incorrect)

My uncle is abroad. (correct)

I look forward to meet you all during the programme. (incorrect)

I look forward to meeting you all during the programme. (correct)

A number of people are well-known by MLA of our constituency. (incorrect)

A number of people are well-known to the MLA of our constituency. (correct)

My neighbour visits his relatives on alternative months. (incorrect)

My neighbour visits his relatives on alternate days. (correct)

Communication skills can be developed by means of continuous practise. (incorrect)

Communication skills can be developed by means of constant practice. (correct)

My friend prefers coffee than tea. (incorrect)

My friend prefers coffee to tea. (correct)

He is superior than me. (incorrect)

He is superior to me. (correct)

Time and tide waits for no man. (incorrect)

Time and tide wait for none. (correct)

A book I read yesterday night was quite interesting. (incorrect)

The book I read last night was quite interesting. (correct)

I asked the candidate which was his native place. (incorrect)

I asked the candidate which his native place was. (correct)

Where did you obtain these informations from? (incorrect)

Where did you obtain these information from? (correct)

Many of our students go to their native places on alternative days. (incorrect)

Many of our students go to their native places on alternate days. (correct)

Charles wishes to avail for one half days leave. (incorrect)

Charles wishes to avail of leave for one- and-a-half days. (correct)

Besides a good knowledge of English, Roger also knows six languages. (incorrect)

Besides a good knowledge of English, Roger knows six languages. (correct)

He is inferior than his cousin. (incorrect)

He is inferior to his cousin. (correct)

Lal prefers coffee than tea. (incorrect)

Lal prefers coffee to tea. (correct)

The police are investigating into the murder case now. (incorrect)

The police are investigating the murder case now. (correct)

Are you understanding what I teach you now? (incorrect)

Do you understand what I am teaching you now? (correct)

The box is too heavy to carry. (incorrect)

The box is too heavy for one to carry. (correct)

Varun joined duty in the forenoon of today. (incorrect)

Varun joined duty on the forenoon of today. (correct)

I like Kamal's action in his new movie. (incorrect)

I like Kamal's acting in his new movie. (correct)

Suraj as well as his sister have joined the GRE course. (incorrect)

Suraj as well as his sister has joined the GRE course. (correct)

He asked his guest how long will he stay in his house? (incorrect)

He asked his guest how long he would stay in his house. (correct)

No other flower is so beautiful as red rose in my garden. (incorrect)

No other flower in my garden is so beautiful as red rose. (correct)

I know Dr Albert since 2001. (incorrect)

I have known Dr Albert since 2001. (correct)

The problem still remains unsolved. (incorrect)

The problem remains unsolved. (correct)

Gardeners are only allowed to enter the garden. (incorrect)

Only gardeners are allowed to enter the garden. (correct)

The speaker got exhausted as he talked continually for seven hours. (incorrect)

The speaker got exhausted as he was talking continuously for seven hours. (correct)

The foreigners exclaimed that the Dal Lake was beautiful. (incorrect)

The foreigners exclaimed that the Dal Lake was very beautiful. (correct)

Balu loosed his temper when he was criticized publicly. (incorrect)

Balu lost his temper when he was criticized publicly. (correct)

The beautiful picture was hanged in the front hall. (incorrect)

The beautiful picture was hung in the front hall. (correct)

He has been named with his grandfather's name. (incorrect)

He has been named after his grandfather. (correct)

Our new principal insists in maintenance of discipline and decorum on the school campus. (incorrect)

Our new Principal insists on maintenance of discipline and decorum on the school campus.

The gardeners are watering on the plants now. (incorrect)

The gardeners are watering the plants now. (correct)

The GM asked to his peon to keep all the files in his table. (incorrect)

The GM asked his peon to keep all the files on his table. (correct)

Joe and Joel are the supporting staff of our office. (incorrect)

Joe and Joel are the support staff of our office. (correct)

If you go to European countries, you will have to pay a big amount on boarding and lodging. (incorrect)

If you go to European countries, you will have to pay a huge amount on board and lodging. (correct)

The team leader is looking forward to meet all the members. (incorrect)

The team leader is looking forward to meeting all the members. (correct)

The secretary forgot to remain the Director of the programme he has today. (incorrect)

The secretary forgot to remind the Director of the programme that he has today. (correct)

Many of friends are leaving to Mumbai now. (incorrect)

Many of my friends are leaving for Mumbai now. (correct)

The teacher asked the student why he did not attend his classes last week. (incorrect)

The teacher asked the student why he had not attended his classes the previous week. (correct)

Can you pinpoint exactly some of the flaws in the system? (incorrect)

Can you pinpoint some of the flaws in the system? (correct)

The problem that they discussed last month still remains unsolved. (incorrect)

The problem that they discussed last month remains unsolved. (correct)

By the time we reach the auditorium, the programme will start. (incorrect)

By the time we reach the auditorium, the programme will have started.

The officer goes to Madurai to attend some personal work. (incorrect)

The officer goes to Madurai to attend to some personal work. (correct)

Your new plans are quite innovative. (incorrect)

Your plans are quite innovative. (correct)

The forward to my book has been given by the MP of our Constituency. (incorrect)

The foreword to my book has been given by the MP of our Constituency. (correct)

The glass jar got broken into piece pieces when the child tried to catch it. (incorrect)

The glass jar got broken into pieces when the child tried to catch it. (correct)

The police caught the thief last night and they have been searching for him for the past seven years. (incorrect)

The police caught the thief last night and they had been searching for him for the past seven years. (correct)

Lavanya is brilliant amidst all her classmates. (incorrect)

Lavanya is brilliant among all her classmates. (correct)

The teacher asked him why did he not upload the assignments on time? (incorrect)

The teacher asked him why he had not uploaded the assignments on time. (correct)

PROOFREADING -EXERCISE

Proofread the following passage:

DR Arnold is working in Oxford university for past twentyfive years. The Area of his intrest and specialization are English language teaching (ELT). His contributions to ELT is commandable. Many a book in ELT have been authored and coauthord by Arnold. He produced 65 phd scholars so for. He insists on all language teachers to employ innovative approaches and method in classroom and to look for bets practises to making teaching learning as much effectively as possible. He has conducted a number of seminars and conferences in English in many nations. In his visit to india in 2007 he had met students of few indian universities and addressed them in many topics related to ELT. Learners in all level of proficiency with English and taechers find his books in ELT as most beneficial. According to DR.Arnold, language learming is not similar to construction of a building but similar to the growth of a planet. Learners in any circumstance should not be discouraged in language learning process. Continuous practise and love in language and literature he emphasize are most essential to enhance language skill. DR Arnold next plan is apply for funded project to enable learners coming from rural and tribal areas to speak English fluently. His aim is to make all the learners who come from rural and tribal areas to compete with all the learners who come from cities.

9 798889 415184 7